W9-ASO-519

OHIO DOMINICAN
COLLEGE LIBRARY
COLUMBUS, OHIO
43219

OHIO DOMINICAN COLLEGE LIBRARY
COLUMBUS, OHIO 43219

The other side of a poem

The other side of a poem

Edited by Barbara Abercrombie

Art by Harry Bertschmann

HARPER & ROW, PUBLISHERS
New York, Hagerstown, San Francisco, London

J
811.5
A

Permissions to reprint the poems and excerpts in this book
appear on the Acknowledgments pages in the back, which
constitute an extension of this copyright page.

The Other Side of a Poem
Copyright © 1977 by Barbara Mattes Abercrombie
All rights reserved. No part of this book may be used or
reproduced in any manner whatsoever without written
permission except in the case of brief quotations embodied
in critical articles and reviews. Printed in the United
States of America. For information address Harper & Row,
Publishers, Inc., 10 East 53rd Street, New York, N.Y. 10022.
Published simultaneously in Canada by Fitzhenry & Whiteside
Limited, Toronto.
First Edition

Designed by Kohar Alexanian

Library of Congress Cataloging in Publication Data
Main entry under title:
The Other side of a poem.

    Includes index.
    SUMMARY: Contemporary American poems grouped
according to the effects they achieve such as
making pictures or music, explaining feelings, or
telling a story.
    1. American poetry—20th century. [1. American
poetry—Collections] I. Abercrombie, Barbara.
PS613.08   811.5'08   76-21394
ISBN 0-06-020028-6
ISBN 0-06-020029-4 lib. bdg.

For Brooke and Gillan

and in memory of their great-grandfather,
James E. Morrisette

107244

Special thanks to: Norma Almquist—teacher, poet, and friend—for her encouragement and advice. And to the children of Lunada Bay Elementary School for their opinions and enthusiasm.

GETTING INTO POETRY

When I was young I didn't like poetry at all. I hated it, as a matter of fact. Either I couldn't understand it, or the poems were about things I didn't care about. Things like robins singing in the spring, or flowers blooming in May. Not that there was anything wrong with robins and flowers—I just didn't find them very interesting.

What I did find interesting were my own feelings—what hurt or felt good, what scared me, what made me laugh. I also was interested in my cat, tadpoles, salamanders, getting mail, secrets, water, summer, and not making a fool of myself. But poets didn't seem to write poems about those things.

Later on I discovered poets who did write about feelings and the things I cared about. (Actually, when you grow up, the things you care about don't change that much. I'm still interested in my cat, getting the mail, secrets, etc.) The poetry they wrote was for grown-ups, though, so everybody thought of it as "Adult Poetry" and most children never got a chance to read it. Which was a shame because a lot of the poets were writing poems that children could understand and enjoy.

I thought it would be fun to share the poems I loved with children, and decided that one way to do that would be to give poetry readings in schools. I chose poems and parts of poems that would show that poetry didn't have to be boring or corny or impossible to understand, that a poem could be just as exciting as a story or a song or a picture.

At my first reading I was very nervous. (That's something else that doesn't change when you grow up. First times are still scary.) The class was nervous, too. The teacher had told them to be very polite, and not to ask for a drink of water or for permission to go to the bathroom. I asked them what they thought of poetry.

"We love it," they all answered politely.

I asked them again. "What do you *really* think of poetry?"
Silence.

Finally a brave fellow in the last row said, "I think it stinks."

I told him I knew exactly how he felt because I had once felt the same way. Then I asked the class for a definition of a poem and several children answered, "A poem is something that rhymes." And a few said, "Poems are about nature and love and stuff like that."

So I read poems about vegetable soup and Tarzan and sunglasses and all sorts of unpoetic subjects to show that poems don't always have to be about nature and love. And they don't have to rhyme, either. I read poems about what it's like when you want to cry, and how summer feels, and different ways to look at a radish. Together we explored all the different things a poem can do, and after each poem was read, we talked about our own experiences and feelings.

That was the most important part of the poetry readings—when we reached out and touched each other with words. We talked and got to know one another in the important ways, the deep-down-this-is-how-I-really-feel ways. It is a sad fact that most people don't tell each other often enough how they feel. And this is one of the best things a poem can do. A poem can start you thinking and talking about feelings and subjects that you usually are too shy or embarrassed to discuss. A poem can express feelings that you can't put into words yourself. When a poem is read aloud and discussed with other people, you realize that a lot of others have the same worries and joys and fears and dreams that you have.

This book came out of many poetry readings and discussions. The poems and parts of poems here are all by modern American writers. I hope you enjoy reading them as much as we did, and that you'll go on to read and discover other poems, and maybe even write some of your own.

Barbara Abercrombie

invitations...

Poems can be all kinds of things.
Some poems are invitations—to try
something new or to take a chance.

invitations...

Don't be polite.
Bite in.
Pick it up with your fingers and lick the juice that
    may run down your chin.
It is ready and ripe now, whenever you are.

You do not need a knife or fork or spoon
or plate or napkin or tablecloth.

For there is no core
or stem
or rind
or pit
or seed
or skin
to throw away.

EVE MERRIAM
"How to Eat a Poem"

invitations...

I'm going out to clean the pasture spring;
I'll only stop to rake the leaves away
(And wait to watch the water clear, I may):
I shan't be gone long.—You come too.

I'm going out to fetch the little calf
That's standing by the mother. It's so young
It totters when she licks it with her tongue.
I shan't be gone long.—You come too.

ROBERT FROST
"The Pasture"

Come,
Let us roam the night together
Singing.

I love you.

Across
The Harlem roof-tops
Moon is shining.
Night sky is blue.
Stars are great drops
Of golden dew.

Down the street
A band is playing.

I love you.

Come,
Let us roam the night together
Singing.

LANGSTON HUGHES
"Harlem Night Song"

invitations...

CATCH ME!
    I love you, I trust you,
    I love you
CATCH ME!
    catch my left foot, my right
    foot, my hand!
    here I am hanging by my teeth
    300 feet up in the air and
CATCH ME!
    here I come, flying without wings,
    no parachute, doing a double triple
    super flip-flop somersault
    RIGHT UP THERE WITHOUT A
    SAFETY NET AND
CATCH ME!
    you caught me!
    I love you!

now it's *your* turn

LENORE KANDEL
from "Circus"

invitations...

Come
With
Me.
Into my garden
Draped with Spanish moss, honeysuckle and wisteria
And I will
Raise you up and lead you on
And I will tell you
A Tale
In a whisper
A tale of Africa and
India
A tale of the Arapaho Indians
A tale of
Scotland and Wales

BARBARA CHASE-RIBOUD
from "Come With Me"

tell a story, make you laugh...

A poem can tell a story that makes you ask
"What happens next?" A poem can make
you smile or giggle or even laugh out loud.

tell a story, make you laugh...

Isabel met an enormous bear;
Isabel, Isabel, didn't care.
The bear was hungry, the bear was ravenous,
The bear's big mouth was cruel and cavernous.
The bear said, Isabel, glad to meet you,
How do, Isabel, now I'll eat you!
Isabel, Isabel, didn't worry;
Isabel didn't scream or scurry.
She washed her hands and she straightened her hair up,
Then Isabel quietly ate the bear up.

OGDEN NASH
from "Adventures of Isabel"

tell a story, make you laugh...

Patrick Casey is sitting on the beach.
Patrick Casey is surrounded by sunshine.
Patrick Casey has a sunny disposition.
Patrick Casey is saying "Ouch!"
There is too much sunshine on this beach.
It is pinching Patrick Casey.

JACK ANDERSON
from "This is a Poem for Patrick Casey"

tell a story, make you laugh...

I had finished my dinner
Gone for a walk
It was fine
Out and I started whistling

It wasn't long before

I met a
Man and his wife riding on
A pony with seven
Kids running along beside them

I said hello and

Went on
Pretty soon I met another
Couple
This time with nineteen
Kids and all of them
Riding on
A big smiling hippopotamus

I invited them home

KENNETH PATCHEN
"An Easy Decision"

12

tell a story, make you laugh...

There once was a girl named Myrtle
Who, strangely enough, *was* a Turtle:
She was mad as a Hare,
She could growl like a Bear, —
O *Nobody* understood Myrtle!

She would sit with a Book on her Knees, —
My Poetry-Book, if you please, —
She'd Rant and She'd Roar:
"This stuff is a Bore!
Why I could do better
With only ONE Letter, —
These Poets, they write like *I* Sneeze!"

THEODORE ROETHKE
"Myrtle"

tell a story, make you laugh...

Jane Lee told me that in Maine she met a little boy who insisted that in his family they had green blood in their veins.

When his mother heard about what he'd said, she spanked him.

But I believe him.

JAMES WRIGHT
"What is Truth?"

What did Tarzan know. He'd lived alone for thirty four years
and then all of a sudden this female dropped out of the sky and
made him build a treehouse. In the daytime she ordered
    him around
and at night she mumbled to him in a language he couldn't
    understand.

"Darling," she said. "My noble savage. You've got so much
    to give.
Call me Jane and get a haircut, won't you?"

RONALD KOERTGE
from "Tarzan"

14

ordinary things...

Poetry can be written about the most
ordinary things in the world. Everyday
things like Campbell's soup and grilled
cheese sandwiches and sunglasses and
peeling apples. Because sometimes
ordinary things are the most important
of all.

ordinary things...

Pause before anything ordinary
       and it becomes important

MICHAEL BROWNSTEIN
"Poem in Two Parts"

Tonight I sat on my back porch
and drank a bowl of
Campbell's chicken vegetable soup.
All that time watching the moon
and feeling absolutely great.

EUGENE LESSER
from "Sometimes Life is Not
a Literary Experience"

ordinary things...

I mean, I just slept
I awoke with a fly on my elbow and
I named the fly Benny
then I killed him
and then I got up and looked in the
mailbox
and there was some kind of warning from the
government
but since there wasn't anybody standing in the bushes with
a bayonet
I tore it up
and went back to bed and looked up at the ceiling
and I thought, I really like this,
I'm just going to lie here for another ten
minutes
and I lay there for another ten minutes
and I thought,
it doesn't make sense, I've got so many things to
do but I'm going to lie here another
half hour,
and I stretched
          stretched

CHARLES BUKOWSKI
from "living"

ordinary things...

One day the Nouns were clustered in the street.
An Adjective walked by, with her dark beauty.
The Nouns were struck, moved, changed.
The next day a Verb drove up, and created the Sentence.

KENNETH KOCH
from "Permanently"

ordinary things...

good evening
    the time is now 5:55 pm
    and I think
    someone's grilled cheese
    has just been burned
    in walgreen's, thank you
    also it won't be considered rude
    if person who waited
    dumps bowl of soup
    on waiter's head, thank you

RITA VALENTINO
from untitled poem

ordinary things...

I sit here dreaming
long thoughts of California

at the end of a November day
below a cloudy twilight
    near the Pacific

listening to The Mamas and The Papas
    THEY'RE GREAT

singing a song about breaking
somebody's heart and digging it!

I think I'll get up
and dance around the room.

    Here I go!

RICHARD BRAUTIGAN
"Our Beautiful West Coast Thing"

ordinary things...

The air is interesting
My sunglasses today.
Last week they were

Interested by the sea.
In my sunglasses
I look like Grandma Moses

Wearing sunglasses
And interested by the sun,
The air, and the sea.

TOM CLARK
from "Sunglasses"

ordinary things...

My Grandmother at her farm table
Would scrape an apple with a pen-knife,
Paring the skin in red curls
    Round and round,
Before scooping up the juice meat,
I never could get the art of it
But far from the orchards
    Above Lake Erie,
From her farm kitchen
    With its bowl of apples,
I try for the red curls

EMILIE GLEN
"Apple Scoop"

delicious sounds...

Poems can have delicious sounds that you
can taste and roll around in your mouth like
Life Savers. Some words prickle your tongue
like Red Hots. Other words are cool and
slippery like Jell-O. Sometimes words slide
and melt together like hot fudge over ice
cream. Or crack and pop like bubble gum.

delicious sounds...

a flock of birds, soaring, twisting, turning,
floating, lifting, swooping, landing, splitting into
pieces (individual birds) that can peck peck peck
before they once again unite in the flock that, rising,
goes reeling, shifting, flying (flying, that's the word
I was looking for) right out of sight.

ANN DARR
"Love Is"

Many-maned scud-thumper, tub
of male whales, maker of worn wood, shrub-
ruster, sky-mocker, rave!
portly pusher of waves, wind-slave.

JOHN UPDIKE
"Winter Ocean"

24

delicious sounds...

I've an ingle, shady ingle, near a dusky bosky dingle
Where the sighing zephyrs mingle with the purling of the
    stream.
There I linger in the jungle, and it makes me thrill and
    tingle,
Far from city's strident jangle as I angle, smoke and dream.

NEWMAN LEVY
from "Midsummer Jingle"

Eskimos in Manitoba,
    Barracuda off Aruba,
Cock an ear when Roger Bobo
    Starts to solo on the tuba.

Men of every station—Pooh-Bah,
    Nabob, bozo, toff, and hobo—
Cry in unison, "Indubi-
    Tably, there is simply nobo-

Dy who oompahs on the tubo
Solo, quite like Roger Bubo!"

JOHN UPDIKE
"Recital"

delicious sounds...

How instant joy, how clang
And whang the sun, how
Whoop the sea, and oh,
Sun, sing, as whiter than
Rage of snow, let sea the spume
Fling.

Let sea the spume, white, fling,
White on blue wild
With wind, let sun
Sing, while the world
Scuds, clouds boom and belly,
Creak like sails, whiter than,
Brighter than,
Spume in sun-song, oho!
The wind is bright.

ROBERT PENN WARREN
*from "Mediterranean Beach,
Day after Storm"*

poems make pictures...

Bit an apple on its red
side   Smelled like snow
Between white halves broken open
brown winks slept in sockets of green

MAY SWENSON
from "Green Red Brown and White"

The telephone poles
Have been holding their
Arms out
A long time now
To birds
That will not
Settle there
But pass with
Strange cawings

DONALD JUSTICE
from "Crossing Kansas
by Train"

poems make pictures...

A woman, sitting and sewing in south window light,
Is silent, and so is the small granddaughter by her side,
Counting not stitches, no, but yellow and red and white
Buttons, and silver snaps, and ribbons fit for a bride.

MARK VAN DOREN
"Morning Assignment"

The neighbour sits in his window and plays the flute.
From my bed I can hear him,
And the round notes flutter and tap about the room,
And hit against each other,
Blurring to unexpected chords.
It is very beautiful,
With the little flute-notes all about me,
In the darkness.

AMY LOWELL
from "Music"

poems make pictures...

A big young bareheaded woman
in an apron

Her hair slicked back standing
on the street

One stockinged foot toeing
the sidewalk

Her shoe in her hand. Looking
intently into it

She pulls out the paper insole
to find the nail

That has been hurting her

WILLIAM CARLOS WILLIAMS
"Proletarian Portrait"

poems make pictures...

The sun hangs
medals,
    bright, pompous, golden
      medals

on the grass,
    which
      stands

green and tall
    in a million
      million

ranks across the yard.

        ROBERT WALLACE
      from "First Dandelions"

The jukebox has a big square face,
A majestic face, softly glowing with red and green and purple
    lights.
Have you got a face as bright as that?

BUT IT'S A PROVEN FACT THAT A JUKEBOX HAS
    NO EARS.

        KENNETH FEARING
      from "King Juke"

music with words...

A poem can be music with words instead
of notes. It can have rhythm and a beat you
can snap your fingers and tap your feet to.
Or it might even make you feel like dancing.

music with words...

The shape of a rat?
> It's bigger than that.
> It's less than a leg
> And more than a nose,
> Just under the water
> It usually goes.

> Is it soft like a mouse?
> Can it wrinkle its nose?
> Could it come in the house
> On the tips of its toes?

> Take the skin of a cat
> And the back of an eel,
> Then roll them in grease,—
> That's the way it would feel.

> It's sleek as an otter
> With wide webby toes
> Just under the water
> It usually goes.

> > THEODORE ROETHKE
> > *from "The Lost Son"*

music with words...

Now touch the air softly,
Step gently. One, two...
I'll love you till roses
Are robin's-egg blue;
I'll love you till gravel
Is eaten for bread,
And lemons are orange,
And lavender's red....

I'll love you till Heaven
Rips the stars from his coat,
And the Moon rows away in
A glass-bottomed boat;
And Orion steps down
Like a diver below,
And Earth is ablaze,
And Ocean aglow.

WILLIAM JAY SMITH
from "A Pavane for the Nursery"

music with words...

The Naming of Cats is a difficult matter,
    It isn't just one of your holiday games;
You may think at first I'm as mad as a hatter
    When I tell you, a cat must have THREE DIFFERENT NAMES.
First of all, there's the name that the family use daily,
    Such as Peter, Augustus, Alonzo or James,
Such as Victor or Jonathan, George or Bill Bailey—
    All of them sensible everyday names.
There are fancier names if you think they sound sweeter,
    Some for the gentlemen, some for the dames:
Such as Plato, Admetus, Electra, Demeter—
    But all of them sensible everyday names.
But I tell you, a cat needs a name that's particular,
    A name that's peculiar, and more dignified,
Else how can he keep up his tail perpendicular,
    Or spread out his whiskers, or cherish his pride?
Of names of this kind, I can give you a quorum,
    Such as Munkustrap, Quaxo, or Coricopat,
Such as Bombalurina, or else Jellylorum—
    Names that never belong to more than one cat.
But above and beyond there's still one name left over,
    And that is the name that you never will guess;
The name that no human research can discover—
    But THE CAT HIMSELF KNOWS, and will never confess.

When you notice a cat in profound meditation,
    The reason, I tell you, is always the same:
His mind is engaged in a rapt contemplation
    Of the thought, of the thought, of the thought of his name:
        His ineffable effable
        Effanineffable
Deep and inscrutable singular Name.

T.S. ELIOT
"The Naming of Cats"

music with words...

Here he played...
        with a boom-a-lang-a-boogie
        and a boom-a-lang-a-woogie
        with a rub-a-dub-dub
        a pi-ya-na for a tub
Whacha *call* that, man? What, man? *That*, man!
Noise like someone rollin' bowlin' balls in a vat
Noise like flock o' locomotives loose on a grade
Call that music, man? Mr. Pine Top spat
On his hands like he was gonna pound
Them ivories with a spade.
Call it sumpin' in between a stampede and a shout
Call it sumpin' lets a glory in the blood git out
Call it boogie woogie. Mr. Pine Top calls it that.

ANNEMARIE EWING
from "Pine Top Smith"

a special view of the world...

A poem can give you a special view of your
world through the eyes of a poet. A view
that will make you look at your world in a
different way. Perhaps make you love
and appreciate it more. Or maybe—just
make you think about it.

a special view of the world...

Outside my window
two tall witch-elms
toss their inspired
green heads in the sun
and lean together
whispering.

Trees make the world
a proper place.

ROBERT NYE
"A Proper Place"

When we are in love, we love the grass,
And the barns, and the lightpoles,
And the small mainstreets abandoned all night.

ROBERT BLY
"Love Poem"

a special view of the world...

Green Buddhas
On the fruit stand.
We eat the smile
And spit out the teeth.

CHARLES SIMIC
"Watermelons"

in the blue night
frost haze, the sky glows
with the moon
pine tree tops
bend snow-blue, fade
into sky, frost, starlight.
the creak of boots.
rabbit tracks, deer tracks,
what do we know.

GARY SNYDER
"Pine Tree Tops"

a special view of the world...

Birds are flowers flying
and flowers perched birds.

A. R. AMMONS
"Mirrorment"

love is a place
& through this place of
love move
(with brightness of peace)
all places

yes is a world
& in this world of
yes live
(skilfully curled)
all worlds

e.e. cummings
"love is a place"

a special view of the world...

Sleep is the gift of many spiders
The webs tie down the sleepers easy.

CARL SANDBURG
"Drowsy"

once upon a time
a freeway came through my life
i walked outside to mail a letter
and the street had walls

EDWARD CARDINALI
"freeway"

43

a special view of the world...

An Owl winks in the shadow
A lizard lifts on tiptoe
            breathing hard
The whales turn and glisten
            plunge and
Sound, and rise again
Flowing like breathing planets

In the sparkling whorls

Of living light.

GARY SNYDER
from "Mother Earth:
Her Whales"

how you feel...

A poem can be a way of explaining how you
feel without arguing or getting mad or feeling silly.

how you feel...

I am a mixture of feelings without beginning
or ending,
a pinch of this,
               a pinch of that.
I'm a horse with an army in my belly
and a rowboat.

JOHN PERREAULT
from "The Mixture"

Oh, on an early morning I think I shall live forever!
I am wrapped in my joyful flesh,
As the grass is wrapped in its clouds of green.

ROBERT BLY
from "Poem in Three Parts"

how you feel...

I have eaten
the plums
that were in
the icebox

and which
you were probably
saving
for breakfast

Forgive me
they were delicious
so sweet
and so cold

WILLIAM CARLOS WILLIAMS
   "This is Just to Say"

how you feel...

Your eyes are just
like bees, and I
feel like a flower.

MAY SWENSON
from "Four-Word Lines"

You feel heavy and sad as though
someone was building a mound
of animal skulls inside you.
Wanting to cry,
you hold your head in your hands;
no tears fall, but even so
when you lift your head
the table is covered
with white snails of kleenex.

GREGORY ORR
from "Domestic Life"

how you feel...

once a snowflake fell
on my brow and i loved
it so much and i kissed
it and it was happy and called its cousins
and brothers and a web
of snow engulfed me then
i reached to love them all
and i squeezed them and they became
a spring rain and i stood perfectly
still and was a flower

NIKKI GIOVANNI
"Winter Poem"

there is a frame around my
words there is a frame around
me that frame is gladness i put
it there for you to see

JUDITH JOHNSON SHERWIN
from "The Frame"

how you feel...

The tulips are too excitable, it is winter here.
Look how white everything is, how quiet, how snowed-in.
I am learning peacefulness, lying by myself quietly
As the light lies on these white walls, this bed, these hands.

SYLVIA PLATH
from "Tulips"

how you feel...

Once,
I was afraid of dying
In a field of dry weeds.
But now,
All day long I have been walking among damp fields,
Trying to keep still, listening
To insects that move patiently.
Perhaps they are sampling the fresh dew that gathers slowly
In empty snail shells
And in the secret shelters of sparrow feathers fallen on the
    earth.

JAMES WRIGHT
"I Was Afraid of Dying"

how you feel...

this morning
this morning
                    i met myself
coming in

a bright
jungle girl
shining
quick as a snake
a tall
tree girl a
me girl
                    i met myself
this morning
coming in

and all day
i have been
a black bell
ringing
i survive
                    survive
survive

                    LUCILLE CLIFTON
                    "this morning"

discoveries...

Some poems are discoveries. You learn
things from them the same way you can
learn things from special people, growing a
garden, walking down the street all by
yourself, or just looking up at the sky.

discoveries...

I met a genius on the train
today
about 6 years old,
he sat beside me
and as the train
ran down along the coast
we came to the ocean
and then he looked at me
and said,
it's not pretty.

it was the first time I'd
realized
that.

CHARLES BUKOWSKI
"i met a genius"

discoveries...

What is once loved
You will find
Is always yours
From that day.
Take it home
In your mind
And nothing ever
Can take it away.

ELIZABETH COATSWORTH
"What is Once Loved"

When I carefully consider the curious habits of dogs
I am compelled to conclude
That man is the superior animal.

When I consider the curious habits of man
I confess, my friend, I am puzzled.

EZRA POUND
"Meditatio"

discoveries...

Look out how you use proud words.
When you let proud words go, it is
    not easy to call them back.
They wear long boots, hard boots; they
    walk off proud; they can't hear you
    calling—
Look out how you use proud words.

CARL SANDBURG
"Primer Lesson"

poems like dreams...

light keeps on breaking.
i keep knowing
the language of other nations.
i keep hearing
tree talk
water words
and i keep knowing what they mean.
and light just keeps on breaking.
last night
the fears of my mother came
knocking and when i
opened the door
they tried to explain themselves
and i understood
everything they said.

LUCILLE CLIFTON
"Breaklight"

poems like dreams...

He watered the roses.
His thumb had a rainbow.
The stems said, Thank you.

THEODORE ROETHKE
from "Where Knock
is Open Wide"

Just now,
Out of the strange
Still dusk...as strange, as still...
A white moth flew. Why am I grown
So cold?

ADELAIDE CRAPSEY
"The Warning"

poems like dreams...

I keep my parents in a garden
among lumpy trees, green sponges
on popsickle sticks. I give them a lopsided
sun which drops its heat
in spokes the colour of yellow crayon.

They have thick elephant legs,
quills for hair and tiny heads;
they clump about under the trees
dressed in the clothes of thirty years
ago, on them innocent as plain skin.

MARGARET ATWOOD
from "Eden is a Zoo"

poems like dreams...

I stopped to pick up the bagel
rolling away in the wind,
annoyed with myself
for having dropped it
as it were a portent.
Faster and faster it rolled,
with me running after it
bent low, gritting my teeth,
and I found myself doubled over
and rolling down the street
head over heels, one complete somersault
after another like a bagel
and strangely happy with myself.

DAVID IGNATOW
"The Bagel"

mysteries or puzzles...

Poems can be like mysteries or puzzles—to
read again and again until you figure them out
or feel comfortable with them. A poem can be
like a secret path you want to explore and
see where it goes. Or like a maze—even
if you get lost, it's fun.

mysteries or puzzles...

So.
I am becoming an elephant,
who stands listening to the rain
under great leaves
barely moving at all.

This is the way it happens.

LARRY LEVIS
*"Cool Morning Shower
in Early Spring"*

There is this cave
In the air behind my body
That nobody is going to touch:
A cloister, a silence
Closing around a blossom of fire.
When I stand upright in the wind,
My bones turn to dark emeralds.

JAMES WRIGHT
"The Jewel"

mysteries or puzzles...

I am the magical mouse
I don't eat cheese
I eat sunsets
And the tops of trees
I don't wear fur
I wear funnels
Of lost ships and the weather
That's under dead leaves

I am the magical mouse
I don't fear cats
Or woodsowls
I do as I please
Always
I don't eat crusts
I am the magical mouse
I eat
Little birds—and maidens

That taste like dust

KENNETH PATCHEN
"The Magical Mouse"

mysteries or puzzles...

The day I was born
The birds stopped singing

The day I was born
The birds started singing

Take your pick
While I take mine

MICHAEL BROWNSTEIN
"Children, It's Time"

so much depends
upon

a red wheel
barrow

glazed with rain
water

beside the white
chickens

WILLIAM CARLOS WILLIAMS
"The Red Wheelbarrow"

mysteries or puzzles...

I walk the purple carpet into your eye
carrying the silver butter server
but a truck rumbles by,
        leaving its black tire prints on my foot
and old images   the sound of banging screen doors on
    hot afternoons
       and a fly buzzing over the Kool-Aid spilled on the sink
flicker, as reflections on the metal surface.

DIANE WAKOSKI
from "Inside Out"

mysteries or puzzles...

An open door says, "Come in."
A shut door says, "Who are you?"
Shadows and ghosts go through shut doors.
If a door is shut and you want it shut,
    why open it?
If a door is open and you want it open,
    why shut it?
Doors forget but only doors know what it is
    doors forget.

CARL SANDBURG
"Doors"

secret messages...

Sometimes a poet will write about something
you have thought but couldn't find the words
for. The poem is a secret message saying
"me, too." And you wish you could answer it
and say "I worry about that, too," or "Yes,
I understand. That's the way it is with me."

secret messages...

Remember when you couldn't
buckle your own
overshoe
or tie your own
shoe
or cut your own meat
and the tears
running down like mud
because you fell off your
tricycle?
Remember, big fish,
when you couldn't swim
and simply slipped under
like a stone frog?
The world wasn't
yours.
It belonged to
the big people.

ANNE SEXTON
from "The Fury of Overshoes"

secret messages...

I love the butterflies
but am silent about them

        ALVARO CARDONA-HINE
          "Menashtash"

secret messages...

The man under the bed
The man who has been there for years waiting
The man who waits for my floating bare foot
The man who is silent as dustballs riding the darkness
The man whose breath is the breathing of small white
butterflies

ERICA JONG
from "The Man Under the Bed"

secret messages...

I always like summer
best
you can eat fresh corn
from daddy's garden
and okra
and greens
and cabbage
and lots of
barbecue
and buttermilk
and homemade ice-cream
at the church picnic
and listen to
gospel music
outside
at the church
homecoming
and go to the mountains with
your grandmother
and go barefooted
and be warm
all the time
not only when you go to bed
and sleep

NIKKI GIOVANNI
"Knoxville, Tennessee"

secret messages...

When I was a child
I played by myself in a
corner of the schoolyard
all alone.

I hated dolls and I
hated games, animals were
not friendly and birds
flew away.

If anyone was looking
for me I hid behind a
tree and cried out "I am
an orphan."

And here I am, the
center of all beauty!
writing these poems!
Imagine!

FRANK O'HARA
"Autobiographia Literaria"

secret messages...

"I hate to lose something,"
    then she bent her head
"even a dime, I wish I was dead.
 I can't explain it. No more to be said.
 Cept I hate to lose something."

"I lost a doll once and cried for a week.
 She could open her eyes, and do all but speak.
 I believe she was took, by some doll-snatching-sneak
 I tell you, I hate to lose something."

"A watch of mine once, got up and walked away.
 It had twelve numbers on it and for the time of day.
 I'll never forget it and all I can say
 Is I really hate to lose something."

MAYA ANGELOU
from "No Loser, No Weeper"

I like to have a home life in the house
I like to like whatever I have
I like to put away and take out what I have
I like to spend money...

I like what I like when I do not worry
I do not worry nor am I in a hurry
If I am in a hurry I do not worry
But I do not worry if I do not worry
And there is no worry in a hurry.

GERTRUDE STEIN
from "Afterwards"

children's poems...

Children can write wonderful poems, too.

children's poems...

I'm a rabbit's foot.
I'm glad because I'm soft.
I'm green and 7 years old.
I used to be a vegetarian
Now I'm a rabbit's foot.

SUSAN LEGG
second grade

Mad is like touching the devil
Mad is as hot as fire
Mad is so bad it tastes like liver
Mad is so bad I don't even think
I should write about it.

SHAWN RANDOLPH
second grade

children's poems...

I am a piece of paper
I have gushy gushy comfort
I crackle
A mean bully named hole puncher
and I got in a fight
He punched 3 holes in me
Pssst...some poet just wrote on me

PAUL GREEN
fifth grade

An egg yolk feels
like a bowl of honey.
You should try it sometime.
Sometimes it feels
like little baby rabbits.

MANDY ANN FRIDLEY
third grade

children's poems...

I wonder
how God lives
in heaven,
when the clouds
seem to be collapsing
like broken birds.

JEWELL LAWTON
age 8

children's poems...

I was born nowhere
And I live in a tree
I never leave my tree
It is very crowded
I am stacked up right against a bird
But I won't leave my tree
Everything is dark
No light!
I hear the bird sing
I wish I could sing
My eyes, they open
And all around my house
The Sea
Slowly I get down in the water
The cool blue water
Oh and the space
I laugh swim and cry for joy
This is my home
     For Ever.

JEFF MORLEY
fifth grade
"The Dawn of Me"

INDEX BY POET

ACKNOWLEDGMENTS

The editor and publisher have made every effort to trace the ownership of all copyrighted material in this volume, and believe that all necessary permissions have been secured. If any errors have inadvertently been made, proper corrections will gladly be made in future editions.

Thanks are due to the following authors, publishers, publications, and agents for permission to use the material included:

Atheneum Publishers for "How to Eat a Poem," copyright © 1964 by Eve Merriam, from IT DOESN'T ALWAYS HAVE TO RHYME. Used by permission of Atheneum Publishers.

Black Sparrow Press for "i met a genius" and excerpt from "living," from BURNING IN WATER, DROWNING IN FLAME, copyright © 1974 by Charles Bukowski. Reprinted by permission of Black Sparrow Press, Santa Barbara, California.

Robert Bly for "Love Poem" and excerpt from "Poem in Three Parts," reprinted from SILENCE IN THE SNOWY FIELDS, Wesleyan University Press, copyright © 1962 by Robert Bly, with his permission.

George Braziller, Inc. for "Watermelons" from RETURN TO A PLACE LIT BY A GLASS OF MILK by Charles Simic, copyright © 1974 by Charles Simic. Reprinted with the permission of the publisher.

Edward Cardinali for "freeway," reprinted by permission of the author.

Alvaro Cardona-Hine for "Menashtash" from MENASHTASH, Little Square Review Press.

Columbia University Press for "Children, It's Time" and "Poem in Two Parts," from Michael Brownstein's HIGHWAY TO THE SKY, copyright © 1969 by Michael Brownstein, published for the Frank O'Hara Foundation at Columbia University Press, 1969. By permission of the publisher and the author.

Definition Press for excerpt from "Purpose for Radishes" from NICE DEITY by Martha Baird, copyright, 1955, by Martha Baird.

Delacorte Press/Seymour Lawrence for "Our Beautiful West Coast Thing" excerpted from THE PILL VERSUS THE SPRINGHILL MINE DISASTER by Richard Brautigan, copyright © 1968 by Richard Brautigan; first and third stanzas of "A Pavane for the Nursery" excerpted from NEW AND SELECTED POEMS by William Jay Smith, copyright © 1954 by William J. Smith. Reprinted with the permission of Delacorte Press/Seymour Lawrence.

Doubleday & Company, Inc. for "Myrtle," copyright 1952 by Theodore Roethke; excerpt from "The Lost Son," copyright 1947 by Theodore Roethke; excerpt from "Where Knock is Open Wide," copyright © 1950 by Theodore Roethke; from the book THE COLLECTED POEMS OF THEODORE ROETHKE. Excerpt from "Inside Out," copyright © 1965 by Diane Wakoski, which first appeared in DISCREP-ANCIES AND APPARITIONS, from the book TRILOGY by Diane Wakoski. All reprinted by permission of Doubleday & Company, Inc.

Annemarie Ewing for excerpt from "Pine Top Smith," which originally appeared in 23 CALIFORNIA POETS, copyright 1968 by Ante-Echo Press. Reprinted by permission of the author.

Faber and Faber Ltd. for "The Naming of Cats" By T.S. Eliot. Reprinted by permission of Faber and Faber Ltd. from OLD POSSUM'S BOOK OF PRACTICAL CATS.

Farrar, Straus & Giroux, Inc. for "Morning Assignment" from 100 POEMS by Mark Van Doren, copyright © by Mark Van Doren; "A Proper Place" from DARKER ENDS by Robert Nye, copyright © 1969 by Robert Nye. Reprinted by permission of Farrar, Straus & Giroux, Inc.

Siv Cedering Fox for excerpt from "Hands" from CUP OF COLD WATER, New Rivers Press, copyright © 1973 by Siv Cedering Fox.

Mandy Ann Fridley for "An Egg Yolk."

Emilie Glen for "Apple Scoop," as published in Yes, Volume 5, #2, Winter 1975.

Paul Green for "I am a Piece of Paper."

Grove Press, Inc. for excerpt from "Circus" from WORD ALCHEMY by Lenore Kandel, copyright © 1960, 1966, 1967 by Lenore Kandel; excerpt from "Permanently" from THANK YOU AND OTHER POEMS by Kenneth Koch, copyright © 1962 by Kenneth Koch. Reprinted by permission of Grove Press, Inc.

Harcourt Brace Jovanovich, Inc. for "love is a place," copyright, 1935, by E.E. Cummings, copyright, 1963, by Marion Morehouse, reprinted from COMPLETE POEMS 1913–1962 by E.E. Cummings; "The Naming of Cats" from OLD POSSUM'S BOOK OF PRACTICAL CATS by T.S. Eliot, copyright, 1939, by T.S. Eliot, copyright, 1967, by Esme Valerie Eliot; "Primer Lesson" from SLABS OF THE SUNBURNT WEST by Carl Sandburg, copyright, 1922, by Harcourt Brace Jovanovich, Inc., copyright, 1950, by Carl Sandburg; "Doors" and "Drowsy," from COMPLETE POEMS, copyright, 1950, by Carl Sandburg; "Window" from CHICAGO POEMS by Carl Sandburg, copyright, 1916, by Holt, Rinehart and Winston, Inc., copyright, 1944, by Carl Sandburg. Reprinted by permission of Harcourt Brace Jovanovich, Inc.

Harper & Row, Publishers, Inc. for excerpt from "Sunglasses," copyright © 1967 by Tom Clark, from STONES by Tom Clark; excerpt from "Tulips," copyright © 1962 by Ted Hughes, from ARIEL by Sylvia Plath. Reprinted by permission of Harper & Row, Publishers, Inc.

Hirt Music, Inc. for excerpt from "No Loser, No Weeper" from JUST GIVE ME A COOL DRINK OF WATER 'FORE I DIIIE by Maya Angelou.

Holt, Rinehart and Winston, Publishers for "The Pasture" from THE POETRY OF ROBERT FROST, edited by Edward Connery Lathem, copyright 1939, © 1967, 1969 by Holt, Rinehart and Winston; five lines from "The Man Under the Bed" from FRUITS & VEGETABLES by Erica Jong, copyright © 1968, 1970, 1971 by Erica Mann Jong. Reprinted by permission of Holt, Rinehart and Winston, Publishers.

Houghton Mifflin Company for excerpt from "Music" from THE COMPLETE POET-ICAL WORKS OF AMY LOWELL, copyright 1955 by Houghton Mifflin Company; excerpt from "The Fury of Overshoes" from THE DEATH NOTEBOOKS by Anne Sexton, copyright © 1974 by Anne Sexton. Reprinted by permission of Houghton Mifflin Company.

Olwyn Hughes for excerpt from "Tulips" from ARIEL by Sylvia Plath, published by Faber and Faber, Ltd., London, copyright © 1965 by Ted Hughes.

Indiana University Press for excerpt from "King Juke" from NEW AND SELECTED POEMS by Kenneth Fearing, copyright © 1956 by Kenneth Fearing; excerpt from "The Mixture" by John Perreault, from UNDER THIRTY: FICTION, POETRY, AND CRITICISM OF THE NEW AMERICAN WRITERS, edited by Charles Newman and William A. Henkin, Jr., copyright © 1966, 1967, 1968, 1969. Reprinted by permission of Indiana University Press.

International Creative Management for excerpt from "The Man Under the Bed" from FRUITS & VEGETABLES by Erica Jong, copyright © 1974 by Erica Jong.

Alfred A. Knopf, Inc. for "The Warning" from VERSE by Adelaide Crapsey, copy-right 1922 by Algeron S. Crapsey and renewed 1950 by The Adelaide Crapsey Foundation; "Harlem Night Song," copyright 1926 by Alfred A. Knopf, Inc. and renewed 1954 by Langston Hughes, reprinted from SELECTED POEMS by Langston Hughes; "Autobiographia Literaria," copyright © 1967 by Maureen Granville-Smith, Administratrix of the Estate of Frank O'Hara, reprinted from THE COL-LECTED POEMS OF FRANK O'HARA; "Winter Ocean," copyright © 1960 by John Updike, reprinted from TELEPHONE POLES AND OTHER POEMS by John Updike; "Recital," copyright © 1961 by John Updike, reprinted from TELEPHONE POLES AND OTHER POEMS by John Updike. By permission of Alfred A. Knopf, Inc.

Susan Joan Legg for "I'm a Rabbit's Foot."

Eugene Lesser for excerpt from "Sometimes Life is Not a Literary Experience," as it appeared in A FIRST READER OF CONTEMPORARY AMERICAN POETRY, Charles E. Merrill Publishing Co.

Little, Brown and Company for excerpt from "Eden is a Zoo" from PROCEDURES FOR UNDERGROUND by Margaret Atwood, copyright © 1970 by Oxford Univer-sity Press (Canadian Branch); excerpt from "Adventures of Isabel" from MANY LONG YEARS AGO by Ogden Nash, copyright 1936 by Ogden Nash. Reprinted by permission of Little, Brown and Company.

Macmillan Publishing Co., Inc. for "What is Once Loved You Will Find" from ALICE ALL BY HERSELF by Elizabeth Coatsworth, copyright 1937 by Macmillan Publishing Co., Inc. renewed 1965 by Elizabeth Coatsworth Beston. Reprinted by permission of Macmillan Publishing Co., Inc.

Eva Levy Marshall for excerpt from "Midsummer Jingle" from GAY BUT WISTFUL by Newman Levy.

William Morrow & Company, Inc. for "Love Is" from ST. ANN'S GUT by Ann Darr, copyright © 1970 by Ann Darr; "Knoxville, Tennessee" from BLACK FEELING, BLACK TALK, BLACK JUDGEMENT by Nikki Giovanni, copyright © 1968, 1970 by Nikki Giovanni; "Winter Poem" from MY HOUSE by Nikki Giovanni, copyright © 1972 by Nikki Giovanni. Reprinted by permission of William Morrow & Company, Inc.

New Directions Publishing Corporation for excerpt from "Living" by Denise Levertov from THE SORROW DANCE, copyright © 1966 by Denise Levertov; "An Easy Decision" and "The Magical Mouse," by Kenneth Patchen from COLLECTED POEMS, copyright 1952 by Kenneth Patchen, copyright © 1957 by New Directions Publishing Corp.; "Meditatio" by Ezra Pound from PERSONAE, copyright 1926 by Ezra Pound; "Pine Tree Tops" and excerpt from "Mother Earth: Her Whales," by Gary Snyder from TURTLE ISLAND, copyright © 1972, 1974 by Gary Snyder; "Proletarian Portrait," "This is Just to Say," and "The Red Wheelbarrow," by William Carlos Williams from COLLECTED EARLIER POEMS, copyright 1938 by New Directions Publishing Corp. Reprinted by permission of New Directions Publishing Corporation.

The New York Quarterly for excerpt from "The Frame" by Judith Johnson Sherwin and excerpt from "good evening..." by Rita Valentino. Reprinted by permission from NYQ #16, copyright © 1974 by The New York Quarterly Poetry Review Foundation, Inc.

W.W. Norton & Company, Inc. for "Mirrorment" from COLLECTED POEMS: 1951–1971 by A.R. Ammons, copyright © 1972 by A.R. Ammons. Reprinted by permission of W.W. Norton & Company, Inc.

Gregory Orr for excerpt from "Domestic Life," as it appeared in The Paris Review #60, Winter 1974.

Oxford University Press (Canadian Branch) for excerpt from "Eden is a Zoo" from PROCEDURES FOR UNDERGROUND by Margaret Atwood.

The Paris Review for "What is Truth?" by James Wright, as it appeared in The Paris Review, #62, Summer 1975, copyright © 1975 by The Paris Review, Inc.; excerpt from "This is a Poem for Patrick Casey" by Jack Anderson, as it appeared in The Paris Review, #57, Spring 1974, copyright © 1974 by The Paris Review, Inc.

Shawn Randolph for "Mad is Like Touching the Devil."

Random House, Inc. for excerpt from "Come With Me" from FROM MEMPHIS AND PEKING by Barbara Chase-Riboud, copyright © 1974 by Barbara Chase-Riboud; "this morning" and "Breaklight," from AN ORDINARY WOMAN by Lucille Clifton, copyright © 1974 by Lucille Clifton; "The Dawn of Me" by Jeff Morley from WISHES, LIES, AND DREAMS: TEACHING CHILDREN TO WRITE POETRY by Kenneth Koch and the Students of P.S. 61, copyright © 1970 by Kenneth Koch; excerpt from "Mediterranean Beach, Day after Storm," copyright © 1966 by Robert Penn Warren, reprinted from SELECTED POEMS: NEW AND OLD 1923–1966 by Robert Penn Warren. Reprinted by permission of Random House, Inc.

The Red Hill Press for excerpt from "Tarzan" by Ronald Koertge from ANTHOL-OGY OF L.A. POETS, originally published by The Red Hill Press, Los Angeles & Fairfax.

Simon & Schuster, Inc. for "I wonder..." by Jewell Lawton from MIRACLES, edited by Richard Lewis, copyright © 1966 by Richard Lewis. Reprinted by permission of Simon & Schuster, Inc.

May Swenson for the first four lines of "Green Red Brown and White" and the first three lines of "Four-Word Lines" by May Swenson from TO MIX WITH TIME, copyright © 1963 by May Swenson. Reprinted by permission of the author.

Terrain Gallery for "Confidence" by Martha Baird and "An Unripe Peach" by Rebecca Fein, from PERSONAL AND IMPERSONAL: SIX AESTHETIC REALISTS, copyright © 1942, 1943, 1951, 1953, 1954, 1955, 1956, 1957, 1958, 1959 by Terrain Gallery.

University of Pittsburgh Press for "Cool Morning Shower in Early Spring" from WRECKING CREW by Larry Levis, copyright © 1972 by Larry Levis. Reprinted by permission of the University of Pittsburgh Press.

Robert Wallace for excerpt from "First Dandelions" from VIEWS FROM A FERRIS WHEEL, copyright © 1960 by Robert Wallace.

Wesleyan University Press for "The Bagel," copyright © 1966 by David Ignatow, reprinted from RESCUE THE DEAD; excerpt from "Crossing Kansas by Train," copyright © 1967 by Donald Justice, reprinted from NIGHT LIGHT; "The Jewel" and "I Was Afraid of Dying," copyright © 1962 by James Wright, reprinted from COLLECTED POEMS. By permission of Wesleyan University Press.

Yale University Press for excerpt from "Afterwards" from STANZAS IN MEDITA-TION by Gertrude Stein, copyright © 1956 by Alice B. Toklas.

107244

DATE DUE

OCT 22	MAR 11 '84	APR. 0 4 1994
FEB 28	MAR 30 '85	
NOV 24 '8	APR 15 '85	
DEC 15 '9	DEC 19 '85	MAY 0 5 1996
	MAR 22 '86	NOV 0 4 1997
MAR 0 1 '86 MAR 0 1 '86	APR 1 3 1987	OCT 1 2 1998
MAY 1 4 '86	DEC 2 1 1989	NOV 2 8 1999
OCT 1 1 1982	MAR 2 5 1991	MAY 0 1 2000
NOV 0 5 1983	NOV. 1 4 1992	MAR 1 3 2003
MAR 30 '84 SEP 11 '84 APR 1 3 1987	APR. 1 8 1993	

J
811.5
A
The Other side of a poem.

Ohio Dominican College Library
1216 Sunbury Road
Columbus, Ohio 43219

DEMCO